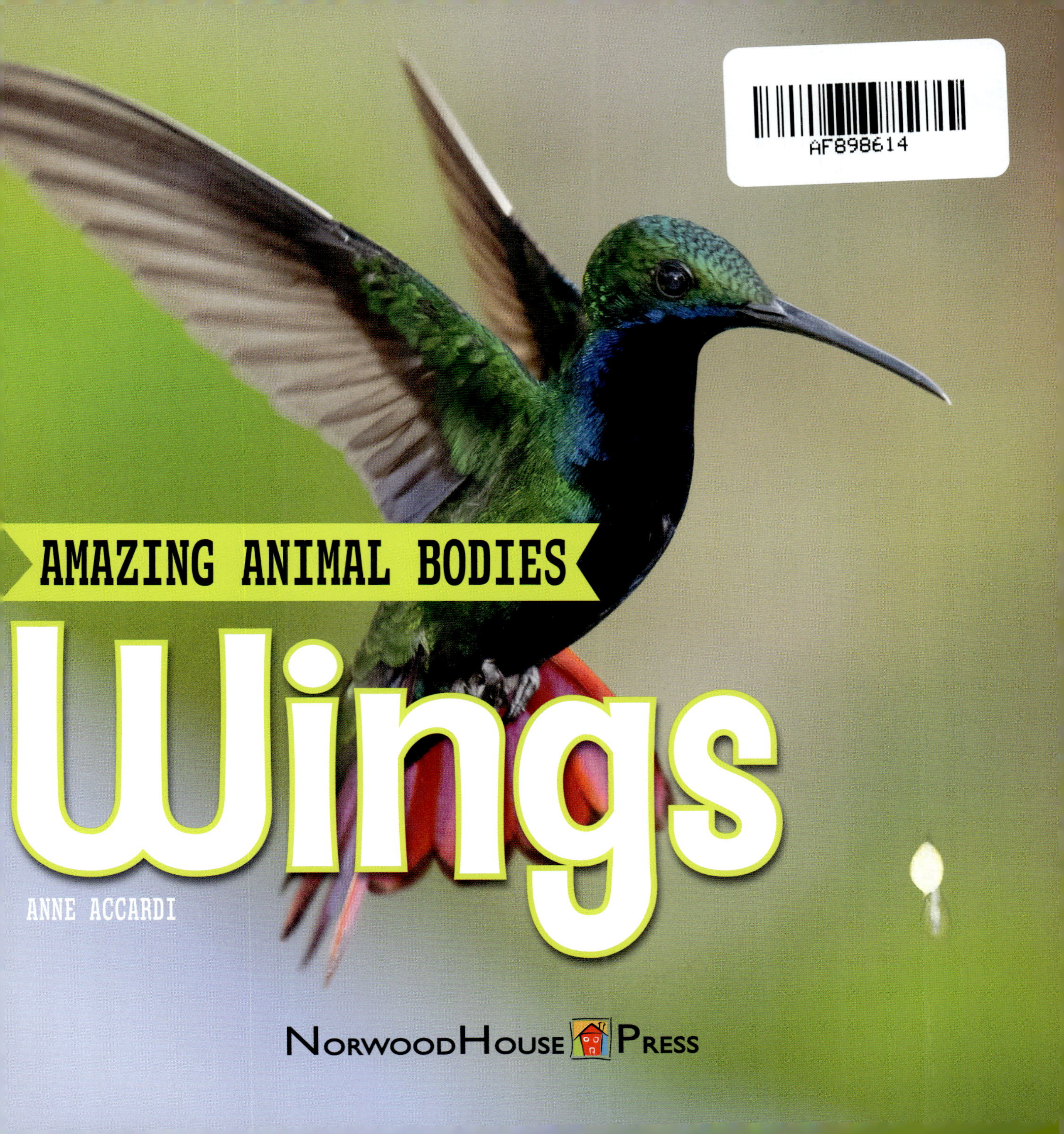

AMAZING ANIMAL BODIES

Wings

ANNE ACCARDI

NorwoodHouse Press

Cataloging-in-Publication Data

Names: Accardi, Anne.
Title: Wings / Anne Accardi.
Description: Buffalo, NY : Norwood House Press, 2027. | Series: Amazing animal bodies | Includes glossary and index.
Identifiers: ISBN 9781978579668 (pbk.) | ISBN 9781978579675 (library bound) | ISBN 9781978579682 (ebook)
Subjects: LCSH: Wings (Anatomy)--Juvenile literature.
Classification: LCC QL950.8 A33 2027 | DDC 591.479--dc23

Published in 2027 by
Norwood House Press
2544 Clinton Street
Buffalo, NY 14224

Designer: Rhea Magaro
Editor: Kim Thompson

Photo credits: Cover, p. 1 Chelsea Sampson/Shutterstock.com; p. 5 Nikky de Graaf/Shutterstock.com; p. 6 Martin Mecrarowski/Shutterstock.com; p. 7 Passakorn Umpornmaha/Shutterstock.com; p. 8 Stephen A. Waycott/Shutterstock.com; p. 9 rck_953/Shutterstock.com; p. 10 Recon Mitra/Shutterstock.com; p. 11 Rudmer Zwerver/Shutterstock.com; p. 13 prochasson frederic/Shutterstock.com; p. 15 Villiers Steyn/Shutterstock.com; p. 16 amirul.photo/Shutterstock.com; p. 17 Cndrej Prosicky/Shutterstock.com; p. 18 Awei/Shutterstock.com; p. 21 Rudmer Zwerver/Shutterstock.com;

Printed in the United States of America

CPSIA compliance information: Batch #CSNHP27: For further information contact Norwood House Press at 1-800-237-9932.

TABLE OF CONTENTS

What Are Wings?

Wings are body parts. They grow from an animal's shoulders.

Most birds and insects have wings.

Wings are thin and flat. Some have bones. Some have **feathers**.

Wings help animals fly!

Robin Wings

A robin flaps its wings. Air above the wings moves faster. Air below is slower. This makes **lift**.

Flapping pushes the bird through the sky. To turn, a robin changes the **angle** of its wings.

Hummingbird Wings

Hummingbirds **hover** in the air as they drink from flowers.

Their wings beat so fast that they look like a blur!

Penguin Wings

Penguins have wings, but they cannot fly. Their wings are **adapted** for swimming. They help penguins "fly" through the water!

Ostrich Wings

The ostrich is another bird that cannot fly. Its wings help it **balance** as it runs on land.

Butterfly Wings

Butterflies have bright, colorful wings. Some have patterns that look like eyes.

A butterfly snaps its wings open. The flash of color scares enemies away!

Beetle Wings

A beetle has two kinds of wings. Hard outer wings protect the **delicate** inner wings. Only the inner wings are used for flying.

Bat Wings

Bats are the only **mammals** with wings. They use their wings to carry babies, trap insects, and do tricks in the air!

Glossary

adapted (uh-DAP-tid): changed over time to fit better in a place or situation

angle (ANG-uhl): how much something is tilted or sloped; a position that is not straight up and down

balance (BAL-uhns): to stay steady and upright

delicate (DEL-i-kit): thin, fine, and easy to break

feathers (FETH-urz): light, soft parts that cover a bird's body

hover (HUHV-ur): to stay in one place in the air

lift (lift): the upward force that overcomes gravity and makes an animal or an airplane rise into the air

mammals (MAM-uhlz): animals that are warm-blooded, have hair or fur, and feed milk to their babies

Thinking Questions

1. Why do birds flap their wings?
2. Why do hummingbirds hover?
3. Name two birds that cannot fly.
4. What is special about butterfly wings?
5. Describe a beetle's wings.

Index

About the Author

Anne Accardi is a librarian who loves reading books and learning new things! She lives in Kansas City, Missouri. When she's not writing, Anne enjoys listening to music, exploring nature around the city, and spending time with her family.